To:

_____

From:

_____

Published by SimpleTruths
1952 McDowell Road
Naperville, Illinois 60563

Design: Lynn Harker, Simple Truths, Illinois

Simple Truths is a registered trademark.
Printed and bound in the United States of America

800-900-3427
www.simpletruths.com

02 WOZ 08

MOTIVATIONAL QUOTES

Compiled by
MAC ANDERSON

$\mathscr{I}$ntroduction

$\mathscr{S}$ince I was a freshman in college, I've loved quotations. The right words can engage the brain and bring an idea to life. With quotes, I've had many "aha" moments, where I've read it and thought, "Wow, that's exactly how I feel!" An idea that was once a "blur" can suddenly become crystal clear.

In 1985, my love of quotes inspired me to publish a small, 80-page quotation book that I called **Motivational Quotes**. At first, the book was offered as a corporate gift, but then we decided to sell it on a plastic easel next to the register, in hotel and airport gift shops. Little did I know what was about to happen. Sales exploded! We couldn't print them fast enough and over the next 18 months, we sold 800,000 copies of the little book pictured:

The light bulb went off when I discovered that many people love quotes as much as I do. I began to wonder...would they want to put quotes on their walls? With this thought, the "big idea" for Successories was born. Our theme, in the beginning was...**Decorate your walls with great ideas**. And I'm pleased to say that millions of customers did just that!

Twenty three years have passed. The book you are holding in your hands is the **new, improved, updated version** of **Motivational Quotes.** It still has my 80 favorite quotes that I introduced in 1985, but I've added 80 more that, since then, have helped to motivate me in good times and bad.

So enjoy this little "treasure of motivation." But here's the key...keep it *close* and read it *often*. Zig Ziglar said it best. He said, "People often say, 'Zig, motivation doesn't last.' And I say to them, 'Bathing doesn't either. That's why I recommend it daily.'"

Live with Passion,

Mac Anderson

No pessimist ever discovered the secrets of the stars, or sailed to an uncharted land, or opened a new doorway for the human spirit.

Helen Keller

Discipline is the bridge between goals and accomplishment.

Jim Rohn

The only thing even in this world are the number of hours in a day. The difference in winning or losing is what you do with those hours.

Woody Hayes

Life offers no guarantees...just choices;
no certainty...but consequences;
no predictable outcomes...just the
privilege of pursuit.

Tim Conner

*I*deas are a dime a dozen.

People who implement them are priceless.

Mary Kay Ash

*P*urpose and laughter are the
twins that must not separate.
Each is empty without the other.

Robert K. Greenleaf

When nothing seems to help, I go and look at
a stonecutter hammering away at his rock
perhaps a hundred times without as much as
a crack showing in it. Yet at the hundred and
first blow it will split in two, and I know
it was not that blow that did it –
but all that had gone before.

Jacob Riis

The bad news is time flies.
The good news is you're the pilot.

Michael Altshuler

A work well begun is half-ended.

Plato

*W*e have committed the
Golden Rule to memory;
let us now commit it to life.

Edwin Markham

Success and failure.
We think of them as opposites,
but they're really not.
They're companions –
the hero and the sidekick.

Laurence Shames

Life is not about waiting for the storms to pass...
it's about learning how to dance in the rain.

Unknown

$\mathcal{T}$he purpose of our lives is to give birth
to the best which is within us.

Marianne Williamson

If a man is called to be a streetsweeper, he should sweep streets even as Michelangelo painted, or Beethoven composed music, or Shakespeare wrote poetry. He should sweep streets so well that all the hosts of heaven and earth will pause to say, here lived a great streetsweeper who did his job well.

Martin Luther King Jr.

I am a great believer in luck,
and I find that the harder I work,
the more I have of it.

Thomas Jefferson

Cherish your dreams,
as they are the children of your soul,
the blueprints of your ultimate achievements.

Napoleon Hill

*S*ometimes our candle goes out,
but is blown into flame by an encounter
with another human being.

Albert Schweitzer

The quality of our expectations
determines the quality
of our actions.

Andre Godin

Knowing thyself is the height of wisdom.

Socrates

Each of us will one day be judged by our standard of life, not by our standard of living; by our measure of giving, not by our measure of wealth; by our simple goodness, not by our seeming greatness.

William A. Ward

Self-respect is the fruit of discipline; and the sense of dignity grows with the ability to say no to oneself.

Abraham Joshua Heschel

Many of life's failures are people who do not realize how close they were to success when they gave up.

Thomas Edison

Anger is a wind which blows out
the lamp of the mind.

Robert G. Ingersoll

Sometimes the best helping hand
you can get is a good, firm push.

Joann Thomas

To be what we are, and to become
what we are capable of becoming,
is the only end in life.

Robert Louis Stevenson

*H*ope arouses, as nothing else can arouse, a passion for the possible.

Rev. William Coffin Jr.

When you have to make a choice and don't make it,
that is in itself a choice.

William James

Feedback is the breakfast of champions.

Rick Tate

Skill to do comes of doing.

Ralph Waldo Emerson

$\mathcal{T}$o get the full value of joy,

you must have someone to divide it with.

Mark Twain

When we have done our best,
we should wait the result in peace.

J. Lubbock

Failure is simply the opportunity to begin again more intelligently.

Henry Ford

The strongest warriors are these two...
time and patience.

Leo Tolstoy

Hope works in these ways:
it looks for the good in people instead of
harping on the worst; it discovers what can
be done instead of grumbling about what
cannot; it regards problems, large or small,
as opportunities; it pushes ahead when it
would be easy to quit; it "lights the candle"
instead of "cursing the darkness."

Anonymous

Give to the world the best you have and
the best will come back to you.

Madeline Bridges

In a moment of decision the best thing you can do is the right thing. The worst thing you can do is nothing.

Theodore Roosevelt

$\mathcal{D}$ucks quack. Eagles soar.

Wayne Dyer

$\mathcal{A}$ pessimist sees the difficulty in every opportunity;

an optimist sees the opportunity in every difficulty.

Winston Churchill

Great minds have purposes, others have wishes.

Washington Irving

Success is not to be pursued;
it is to be attracted by the person you become.

Jim Rohn

$\mathcal{T}$o love what you do and feel that it matters –
how could anything be more fun?

Katharine Graham

Chance favors those in motion.

James H. Austin

When you do the things you have to do when you have to do them, the day will come when you can do the things you want to do when you want to do them.

Zig Ziglar

Very often a change of self is
needed more than a change of scene.

Arthur Christopher Benson

*W*ithout involvement, there is no commitment.
Mark it down, asterisk it, circle it, underline it.
No involvement, no commitment.

Stephen Covey

Destiny is not a matter of chance, it's a matter of choice; it is not a thing to be waited for, it is a thing to be achieved.

William Jennings Bryan

There's no thrill in easy sailing when the skies are clear and blue, there's no joy in merely doing things which any one can do. But there is some satisfaction that is mighty sweet to take, when you reach a destination that you thought you'd never make.

Spirella

Don't be afraid to go out on a limb...
that's where the fruit is.

Harry S. Truman

True greatness is starting where you are, using what you have, doing what you can.

Arthur Ashe

Constant effort and frequent mistakes
are the stepping stones to genius.

Elbert Hubbard

Success without honor is an unseasoned dish; it will satisfy your hunger, but won't taste good.

Joe Paterno

The nose of the bulldog is slanted backwards so he can continue to breathe without letting go.

Winston Churchill

$\mathcal{L}$ife is no straight and easy corridor along which we travel free and unhampered, but a maze of passages, through which we must seek our way, lost and confused, now and again checked in a blind alley. But always, if we have faith, a door will open for us, not perhaps one that we ourselves would ever have thought of, but one that will ultimately prove good for us.

A.J. Cronin

*N*othing in the world can take the place of persistence. Talent will not; nothing is more common than unsuccessful men with talent. Genius will not; unrewarded genius is almost a proverb. Education will not; the world is full of educated failures. Persistence and determination alone are omnipotent.

Calvin Coolidge

Today I will do what others won't,
so tomorrow I can accomplish what others can't.

Jerry Rice

The difference in winning and losing is most often...
not quitting.

Walt Disney

$\mathcal{K}$nowing is not enough;
we must apply.
Wishing is not enough; we must do.

Johann Wolfgang Von Goethe

I can accept failure.
Everyone fails at something.
But I can't accept not trying.

Michael Jordan

Every thought is a seed. If you plant crab apples, don't count on harvesting golden delicious.

Bill Meyer

You can have anything you want in life if you just help enough other people get what they want.

Zig Ziglar

It is never too late to be what
you might have been.

George Eliot

$\mathcal{T}$he will to win is not nearly as important

as the will to prepare to win.

Bobby Knight

Courage is not limited to the battlefield.
The real tests of courage are much quieter.
They are the inner tests, like enduring pain
when the room is empty or standing alone
when you're misunderstood.

Charles Swindoll

Success in any endeavor does not happen
by accident. Rather, it's the result of
deliberate decisions, conscious effort,
and immense persistence...
all directed at specific goals.

Gary Ryan Blair

The harder you work,
the harder it is to surrender.

Vince Lombardi

*M*ost folks are about as happy as they make up their minds to be.

Abraham Lincoln

The most powerful weapon on earth
is the human soul on fire.

Ferdinand Foch

I don't know the key to success, but the key to failure is trying to please everybody.

Bill Cosby

If you can find a path with no obstacles,

it probably doesn't lead anywhere.

Frank A. Clark

*N*o great thing is created suddenly.

Epictetus

Who begins too much accomplishes little.

German Proverb

There are no shortcuts to any place worth going.

Beverly Sills

*W*ake up with a smile and go after life...
Live it, enjoy it, taste it, smell it, feel it..

Joe Knapp

*D*ig the well before you are thirsty.

Chinese Proverb

Anyone can hold the helm when the sea is calm.

Publilius Syrus

Habits are first cobwebs, then cables.

Spanish Proverb

There is a time to let things happen and a

time to make things happen.

Hugh Prather

The best time to plant a tree was 20 years ago.

The next best time is now.

Chinese Proverb

Nobody grows old
by merely living a number of years.
People grow old by deserting their ideals.
You are as young as your faith, as old as your doubt;
as young as your self-confidence, as old as your fear;
as young as your hope, as old as your despair.

Douglas Mac Arthur

Trust yourself.
Create the kind of self that you will
be happy to live with all of your life.
Make the most of yourself by fanning the tiny,
inner sparks of possibility into
flames of achievement.

Golda Meir

When written in Chinese,
the word 'crisis' is composed of two characters –
one represents danger and the other
represents opportunity.

John F. Kennedy

$\mathcal{B}$ehind me is infinite power.
Before me is endless possibility.
Around me is boundless opportunity.
Why should I fear?

Stella Stuart

Failure is not fatal, but failure to change might be.

John Wooden

The highest reward for a person's toil is not what they get for it, but what they become by it.

John Ruskin

Swing hard, in case they throw the
ball where you're swinging.

Duke Snider

Knowledge is power,

but enthusiasm pulls the switch.

Ivern Ball

To carry a grudge is like being stung to death by one bee.

William H. Walton

Choose a job you love, and you will never
have to work a day in your life.

Confucius

A ship in port is safe, but that's not what ships are built for.

Grace Hopper

If you would hit the mark,
you must aim a little above it;
every arrow that flies feels
the attraction of earth.

Henry Wadsworth Longfellow

Kindness is more important than wisdom,
and the recognition of this is
the beginning of wisdom.

Theodore Isaac Rubin

We need to learn to set our course by
the stars, not by the lights
of every passing ship.

General Omar N. Bradley

*T*he heart has reasons which
reason cannot understand.

Blaise Pascal

*S*et peace of mind as your highest goal,

and organize your life around it.

Brian Tracy

A man wrapped up in himself
makes a very small bundle.

Benjamin Franklin

We act as though comfort and luxury were the chief requirements of life, when all that we need to make us really happy is something to be enthusiastic about.

Charles Kingsley

We make a living by what we get.
We make a life by what we give.

Winston Churchill

To be what we are, and to become
what we are capable of becoming,
is the only end of life.

Robert Louis Stevenson

Faith is taking the first step
even when you don't see the staircase.

Martin Luther King, Jr.

Happiness lies in the joy of achievement
and the thrill of creative effort.

Franklin Roosevelt

*U*ltimately we know deeply that the other

side of every fear is freedom.

Marilyn Ferguson

*W*hat lies behind us,

and what lies before us,

are tiny matters compared

to what lies within us.

Ralph Waldo Emerson

Life begins when you do.

Hugh Downs

Do the thing you fear,
and the death of fear is certain.

Ralph Waldo Emerson

What I hear, I forget.
What I see, I remember.
What I do, I know.

Chinese Proverb

We are what we repeatedly do.
Excellence, then, is not
an act but a habit.

Aristotle

The road to *Easy Street* goes through the dump.

John Madden

You'll always miss 100% of the shots you don't take.

Wayne Gretsky

Envisioning the end is enough

to put the means in motion.

Dorothea Brande

$\mathcal{W}$e learn to walk by stumbling.

Bulgarian Proverb

As I grow older,
I pay less attention to what men say.
I just watch what they do.

Andrew Carnegie

Do what you can,
with what you have,
where you are.

Theodore Roosevelt

When patterns are broken,
new worlds emerge.

Tuli Kupferberg

It's our attitude in life that
determines life's attitude toward us.

Earl Nightingale

To dream anything that you want to dream.

That is the beauty of the human mind.

To do anything that you want to do.

That is the strength of the human will.

To trust yourself to test your limits.

That is the courage to succeed.

Bernard Edmonds

The credit belongs to the man who is actually in the arena; whose face is marred by dust and sweat and blood; who strives valiantly; who errs and comes short again and again; who knows the great enthusiasms, the great devotions, and spends himself in a worthy cause/who at the best knows in the end the triumph of high achievement; and who at the worst, if he fails, at least fails daring greatly.

Theodore Roosevelt

Worry often gives a small thing a big shadow.

Swedish Proverb

I attribute my success to this:

I never gave or took an excuse.

Florence Nightingale

I have learned that success is to be measured
not so much by the position that one has reached
in life as by the obstacles which he has had
to overcome while trying to succeed.

Booker T. Washington

Be more concerned with your character than your reputation, because your character is what you really are, while your reputation is merely what others think you are.

John Wooden

Just as iron rusts from disuse,
even so does inaction spoil the intellect.

Leonardo Da Vinci

One can never consent to creep when
one feels an impulse to soar.

Helen Keller

A person's mind stretched to a new idea never goes back to its original dimensions.

Oliver Wendell Holmes

Progress always involves risks.

You can't steal second base and keep your foot on first.

Frederick B. Wilcox

$\mathcal{T}$here is a time for departure even
when there's no certain place to go.

Tennessee Williams

*O*nly passions, great passions,

can elevate the soul to great things.

Denis Diderot

The real voyage of discovery consists
not in making new landscapes
but in having new eyes.

Marcel Proust

Enthusiasm is nothing more or less than faith in action.

Henry Chester

*L*uck is what happens when preparation meets opportunity.

Darrell Royal

A journey of a thousand miles begins within a single step.

Chinese Proverb

Our chief want in life is somebody
who will make us do what we can.

Ralph Waldo Emerson

Life is made of memorable moments.
We must teach ourselves to really live...
to love the journey not the destination.

Ann Quindlen

We cannot become what we need to be by remaining what we are.

Max De Pree

*A*bility is what you're capable of doing.

Motivation determines what you do.

Attitude determines how well you do it.

Lou Holtz

Attitude is the librarian of our past,
the speaker of our present and
the prophet of our future.

John Maxwell

Hope is the thing with feathers that perches in the soul, and sings the tune without the words, and never stops at all.

Emily Dickinson

You can't build a reputation on what
you're going to do.

Henry Ford

*H*ot heads and cold hearts
never solved anything.

Billy Graham

The key is not to prioritize what's on the schedule, but to schedule your priorities.

Stephen Covey

All things are difficult before they are easy.

John Norley

$\mathcal{W}$hether you think you can,

or think you can't...

you're right.

Henry Ford

$\mathcal{E}$nthusiasm is the mother of effort.

Without it, nothing great was

ever achieved.

Ralph Waldo Emerson

Life is an echo; what you send out comes back.

Chinese Proverb

Even if you're on the right track,
you'll get run over if you just sit there.

Will Rogers

*Trifles make perfection,
and perfection is no trifle.*

Michelangelo

The great use of life is to spend it
for something that will outlast it.

William James

There are times when silence has the loudest voice.

Leroy Brownlow

Three grand essentials to happiness in this life
are something to do, something to love,
and something to hope for..

Joseph Addison

*I*t is the nature of man to rise to greatness
if greatness is expected of him.

John Steinbeck

Vision without action is a daydream.

Action without vision is a nightmare.

Japanese Proverb

Motivation is what gets you started.
Habit is what keeps you going.

Jim Ryun

The miracle is this —
the more we share, the more we have.

Leonard Nimoy

About the Author

Mac Anderson is the founder of Simple Truths and Successories, Inc., the leader in designing and marketing products for motivation and recognition. These companies, however, are not the first success stories for Mac. He was also the founder and CEO of McCord Travel, the largest travel company in the Midwest, and part owner/VP of sales and marketing for Orval Kent Food Company, the country's largest manufacturer of prepared salads.

His accomplishments in these unrelated industries provide some insight into his passion and leadership skills. He also brings the same passion to his speaking where he speaks to many corporate audiences on a variety of topics, including leadership, motivation, and team building.

Mac has authored or co-authored nine books: *You Can't Send a Duck to Eagle School, The Nature of Success, The Power of Attitude, The Essence of Leadership, Finding Joy, To a Child, Love is Spelled T-I-M-E, The Dash, 212°: The Extra Degree,* and *Change is Good... You Go First.*

For more information about Mac, **visit www.simpletruths.com**

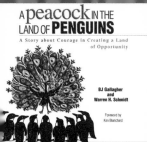
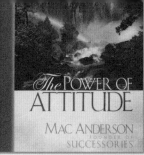
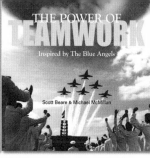
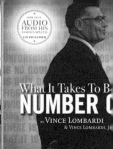

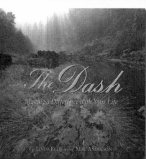
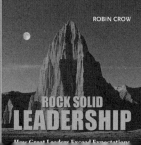